MY FIRST 100 HEBREW WORDS

For Roger,
Sharon,
Danielle,
and Gregory
Goodman,
who give
new meaning
to the word
mishpachah.

Book Design: Giora Carmi

MY FIRST 100 HEBREW WORDS

A YOUNG PERSON'S DICTIONARY OF JUDAISM

HOWARD I. BOGOT
ILLUSTRATED BY GIORA CARMI

UAHC PRESS
NEW YORK, NEW YORK

A

אֲדֹנָי — ADONAI

Adonai is a Hebrew name for God. We can pray to Adonai at home or in the synagogue.

אָלֶף-בֵּית — ALEF-BET

Alef and Bet are the first two letters of the Hebrew alphabet.

עֲלִיָּה — ALIYAH

Aliyah means "to go up." When we are called up to the Torah in the synagogue, we are making an aliyah. When we move to the State of Israel, we are making a different kind of aliyah.

עַם יִשְׂרָאֵל   AM YISRAEL

The Hebrew name for the people of Israel is am Yisrael. All Jews are part of am Yisrael.

אָמֵן   AMEN

We say "amen" at the end of a prayer, showing that we believe what it says.

אֲרוֹן הַקֹּדֶשׁ   ARON HAKODESH

Aron Hakodesh means "Holy Ark." We keep the Torah scrolls in the Aron Hakodesh in the synagogue.

אָבוֹת   AVOT

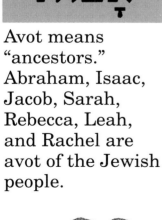

Avot means "ancestors." Abraham, Isaac, Jacob, Sarah, Rebecca, Leah, and Rachel are avot of the Jewish people.

B

בַּר מִצְוָה — BAR MITZVAH

A Jewish boy becomes bar mitzvah when he reaches the age of thirteen. As a bar mitzvah he becomes responsible for performing the commandments of the Torah.

בַּת מִצְוָה — BAT MITZVAH

A Jewish girl who reaches the age of twelve or thirteen becomes bat mitzvah. As a bat mitzvah, she becomes responsible for performing the commandments of the Torah.

בְּרָכָה — BERACHAH

A berachah is a "blessing." When we thank God for something, we are saying a berachah.

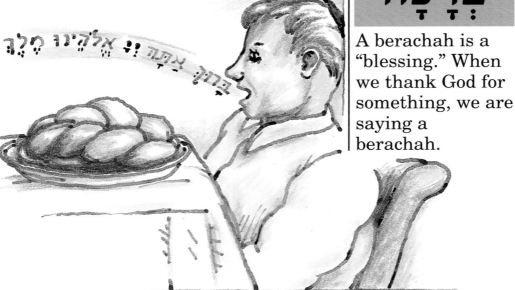

בְּרִית BERIT

A berit is an agreement. The people of Israel has a special berit with God.

בֵּית כְּנֶסֶת BET KNESSET

Bet Knesset means "synagogue." Jews pray, study, and meet friends in the synagogue. Many Jews call their synagogue a temple.

בִּימָה BIMAH

A bimah is a platform in the synagogue. The Aron Hakadosh is usually on the bimah.

בִּרְכַּת הַמָּזוֹן BIRKAT HAMAZON

The Birkat Hamazon is the blessing we sing after eating to thank God for our food.

חַג שָׂמֵחַ **CHAG SAMEACH**

We say "Chag Sameach" to wish our Jewish friends a "happy holiday."

חַלָּה **CHALLAH**

On Shabbat and other Jewish holidays we eat a special kind of bread called challah.

חֲנֻכָּה **CHANUKAH**

Chanukah is a Jewish holiday also known as the "Festival of Lights." We light a candle on each of the eight nights of Chanukah to remember the brave Maccabees and to celebrate freedom.

חֲרֹסֶת CHAROSET

We mix chopped apples, wine, nuts, and spices to make a sweet Pesach food called charoset. We put charoset on the seder plate to remind us of a building material used by the Israelites in ancient Egypt.

חֲבוּרָה CHAVURAH

Chavurah is a group of friends who celebrate, pray, and study together.

חַזָּן CHAZAN

The chazan, or "cantor," sings in the synagogue and helps us pray with music.

חֻמָשׁ CHUMASH

The Five Books of Moses are called the Chumash. The Chumash is part of the Hebrew Bible.

חֻפָּה CHUPAH

At a Jewish wedding the bride and groom stand under a "canopy" called a chupah. It is usually made of cloth and held up by four poles.

D

דַּיֵּנוּ DAYENU

Dayenu is a song of thanks we sing during the Pesach seder.

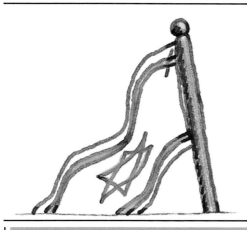

דֶּגֶל DEGEL

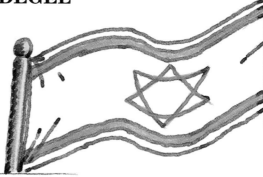

Degel means "flag." The six-pointed star on the degel of the State of Israel is blue.

דֶּרֶךְ אֶרֶץ DERECH ERETZ

When we act in a kind and polite way, we are showing derech eretz toward other people.

דְּבַר תּוֹרָה DEVAR TORAH

A Devar Torah is a short sermon taken from an idea in the Torah. We can learn important lessons from a Devar Torah.

E

אֶתְרוֹג ETROG

An etrog is a fruit that looks like a big lemon. We show an etrog on the holiday of Sukot.

עֵץ חַיִּים ETZ CHAYIM

Etz Chayim means "Tree of Life." The Torah is called Etz Chayim.

G

גְּמַר חֲתִימָה טוֹבָה GEMAR CHATIMAH TOVAH

Between Rosh Hashanah and Yom Kippur, Jews greet one another by saying "Gemar Chatimah Tovah!" It means we wish you a happy future.

H

הַגָּדָה HAGGADAH

The haggadah is a storybook we read at the Pesach seder. It tells how the ancient Israelites escaped from slavery to free-dom.

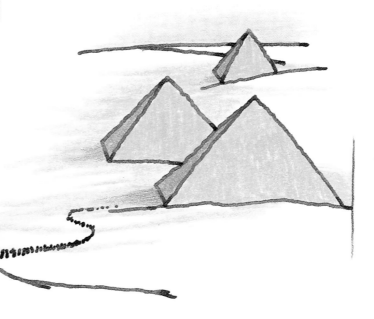

הַמּוֹצִיא HAMOTZI

Hamotzi is the blessing we say or sing before eating.

הַתִּקְוָה HATIKVAH

Hatikvah means "hope." The national anthem of the State of Israel is "Hatikvah."

הַבְדָּלָה HAVDALAH

Havdalah is the prayer we say at the end of the Sabbath to separate Shabbat from the other days of the week. During

Havdalah we sip sweet grape juice or wine, smell spices, and light a special twisted candle.

I

עִבְרִית IVRIT

Ivrit is the Hebrew language. Most of the Torah is written in Ivrit. People who live in Israel speak Ivrit every day.

K

קַבָּלַת שַׁבָּת KABBALAT SHABBAT

Kabbalat Shabbat means "welcoming Shabbat" as a day of prayer, study, and rest. Kabbalat Shabbat comes every Friday evening.

קַדִּישׁ KADDISH

Jews say the Kaddish prayer to praise God, especially at a time when they are remembering a person who has died.

קָדוֹשׁ KADOSH

Kadosh means "holy" or "special." God is kadosh. In the Bible, God asks the Jewish people to be kadosh.

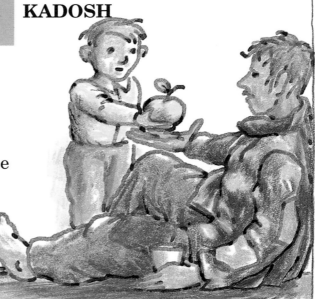

כָּשֵׁר KASHER

Kasher means "proper." According to the Torah, only certain foods are proper for Jews to eat. These foods are kasher or kosher.

כֶּתֶר KETER

Keter means "crown." A Torah scroll is often decorated with a keter.

קִבּוּץ KIBBUTZ

A kibbutz is a community in Israel, where people live, work, eat meals, and make decisions together.

קִדּוּשׁ KIDDUSH

Kiddush is the blessing we say or sing over a cup of wine or grape juice on Shabbat and Jewish holidays.

כִּפָּה   KIPAH

A kipah is a traditional Jewish head covering. Wearing a kipah is a way of showing respect for God.

כָּל הַכָּבוֹד   KOL HAKAVOD

Kol Hakavod means "congratulations." When a person does something very well, we say "Kol Hakavod!"

כָּל נִדְרֵי   KOL NIDRE

Kol Nidre is the prayer we say in the synagogue on the eve of Yom Kippur. During the Kol Nidre prayer we wish one another a good life.

L

לְחַיִּים   **LECHAYIM**

Lechayim means "to life." When we raise a cup of wine or grape juice and say "Lechayim," we wish one another a good life.

לְשָׁנָה טוֹבָה   **LESHANAH TOVAH**

Leshanah Tovah means "to a good year." On Rosh Hashanah, the Jewish New Year, we wish our Jewish friends "Leshanah Tovah!"

לוּלָב   **LULAV**

The lulav is a palm branch tied together with twigs from a willow tree and a myrtle bush. On Sukot, when we shake a lulav in all directions, we are showing that God is everywhere.

M

מָגֵן דָּוִד   **MAGEN DAVID**

The Magen David or the "Star of David," a six-pointed star, is a Jewish symbol in the center of the flag of Israel.

מַלְכָּה   **MALKAH**

Malkah means "queen." We speak of Shabbat as a queen because, like a queen, Shabbat is special.

מָרוֹר   **MAROR**

Maror means "bitter." From the Pesach seder plate we taste a bitter food like horseradish to remember that people who are slaves do not live a sweet life.

מַצָּה MATZAH

Matzah is a flat bread, made without yeast, that looks and tastes like a big cracker. We eat matzah on Pesach to remember that the Jews, escaping from Egypt, did not have time to wait for the dough to rise.

מַזָּל טוֹב MAZAL TOV

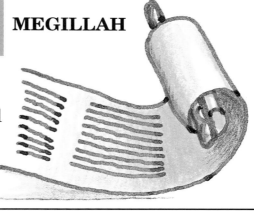

Mazal Tov means "Good Luck!" We say "Mazal Tov" at special times to wish a person luck or congratulations.

מְגִלָּה MEGILLAH

A megillah is a "scroll." Megillat Esther, "the Scroll of Esther," is an important megillah in our Bible.

מְנוֹרָה MENORAH

A menorah is a candleholder. We light candles in a menorah to welcome the Shabbat and other Jewish holidays.

מְזוּזָה MEZUZAH

A mezuzah is a case that holds a tiny scroll with words from the Torah. We attach the mezuzah container, with its scroll inside, to the doorways of our home.

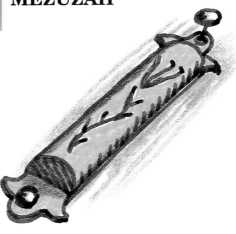

מִנְיָן MINYAN

A minyan is a group of ten Jews who come together for certain prayers.

מִשְׁפָּחָה MISHPACHAH

Mishpachah means "family." The Jewish people is a mishpachah with members living in many lands.

מִצְוָה MITZVAH

A mitzvah is an order from God, telling us what to do to be good people and good Jews.

N

נֵר תָּמִיד   NER TAMID

The Ner Tamid is a light that is kept burning at all times above the Aron Hakodesh in the synagogue.

נֵס   NES

Nes means "miracle." God fills the world and our lives with miracles.

O

עֹנֶג   ONEG

Oneg means "pleasure" or "delight." After we pray in the synagogue on Shabbat, we often eat sweets and talk with friends at a happy gathering called an Oneg.

P

פָּרָשָׁה PARASHAH

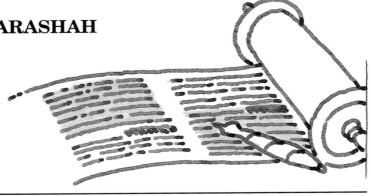

The parashah is the weekly reading from the Torah. Each week we study a different parashah.

פֶּסַח PESACH

Pesach is a Jewish holiday also called "Passover." During Pesach, we eat a special meal and read about our ancestors' escape from slavery in the land of Egypt.

פּוּרִים PURIM

On the joyous holiday of Purim, we dress up in costumes and make noise in the synagogue when the name of the evil Haman is read from Megillat Esther.

R

רַבִּי RABBI

Rabbi means "teacher." A rabbi teaches us about Jewish laws and customs and helps us study and pray in the synagogue.

רֹאשׁ הַשָּׁנָה ROSH HASHANAH

On Rosh Hashanah Jews celebrate the birth of the world. We eat apples dipped in honey on Rosh Hashanah.

S

סֵדֶר SEDER

Seder means "order." Our Pesach meal is called a seder because we tell the Passover story and eat the holiday foods in a special order.

סֵפֶר תּוֹרָה · SEFER TORAH

Sefer Torah means "Book of the Torah." We learn about Judaism when we study lessons from our Sefer Torah.

סְבִיבוֹן · SEVIVON

A sevivon is a spinning toy decorated with four Hebrew letters. On Chanukah we play a game with a sevivon. A sevivon is also called a dreidel.

שַׁבָּת · SHABBAT

Shabbat is the seventh day of the Jewish week. It is the day God rested after creating the world.

Shabbat is a day of rest, but it is also a time for study, prayer, and thoughts about God.

שָׁלַח מָנוֹת · SHALACH MANOT

Shalach Manot are tasty treats we share as gifts with friends and family on Purim.

שָׁלוֹם   SHALOM

Shalom means "peace." Shalom also means "hello" and "goodbye." On Shabbat we say, "Shabbat Shalom," which means "Sabbath of peace."

שָׁבוּעוֹת   SHAVUOT

Shavuot is a Jewish holiday. We celebrate God's giving us the Ten Commandments at Mount Sinai. In the synagogue we study the Ten Commandments and the Scroll of Ruth.

שֶׁהֶחֱיָנוּ   SHEHECHEYANU

Shehecheyanu is a prayer of thanksgiving. We thank God with a Shehecheyanu when we experience something new and wonderful in our lives.

שָׁלוֹם בַּיִת   SH'LOM BAYIT

Shalom means "peace" and bayit means "house." It is important to make our home a sh'lom bayit, a peaceful place.

שְׁמַע SHEMA

Shema means "hear." It is the first word of the most important lesson recited in the synagogue – "Hear, O people of Israel: There is only one God!"

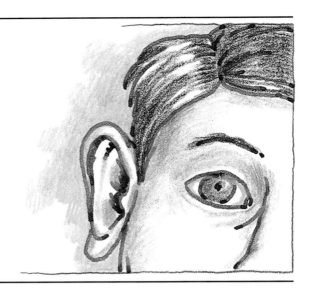

שִׁבְעָה SHIVAH

Shivah means "seven." After a funeral the closest members of the family spend seven days remembering the person who has died. Relatives and friends visit the family to share those special memories.

שׁוֹפָר SHOFAR

A shofar is a ram's horn blown on Rosh Hashanah and at other special times.

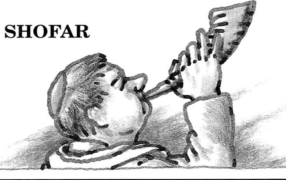

סִדּוּר SIDDUR

Our prayer book is called a siddur. Jews pray from a siddur in the synagogue and at home.

סוֹפֵר — SOFER

The person who writes a Torah scroll is called a sofer.

סֻכָּה — SUKAH

A sukah is a small, fragile building. We eat our meals in a sukah during the holiday of Sukot. We hang fruit and other decorations from the branches that cover the sukah.

סֻכּוֹת — SUKOT

Sukot is a harvest holiday. On Sukot we say blessings of thanksgiving and eat our meals in a sukah.

T

טַלִּית — TALIT

A talit is a prayer shawl with fringes. Many Jews wear a talit when they pray.

תַּלְמוּד TALMUD

The Talmud is a collection of books that teaches us how Jews should behave. The Talmud contains Jewish laws, folk lessons, and opinions about the Bible.

תַּנַ"ךְ TANACH

Tanach is the Hebrew name for the Hebrew Bible. Our Tanach has three parts: Torah, Prophets, and Writings.

תְּפִלָּה TEFILAH

Tefilah means "prayer." We can say or sing a tefilah at home or in the synagogue – anywhere, anytime.

תּוֹרָה TORAH

Torah means "teaching." The first five books of the Hebrew Bible are called the Torah. A Torah scroll is called the Torah. All Jewish study is called Torah.

טְ"וּ בִּשְׁבָט   TU BISHVAT

Tu Bishvat is a Jewish holiday also called the "New Year of the Trees." Tu Bishvat reminds us that we must protect the environment.

צְדָקָה   TZEDAKAH

Tzedakah means "doing the right thing." Giving food and shelter to hungry people is tzedakah. The best kind of tzedakah is helping people help themselves.

U

אוּלְפָּן   ULPAN

An ulpan is a special class in which we learn to speak Hebrew. If we move to Israel, we can study Hebrew in an ulpan.

V

וְאָהַבְתָּ VE'AHAVTA

When we say the Shema, we include a lesson from the Torah that begins with the word

Ve'ahavta. Ve'ahavta teaches us to love God with all our hearts, all our souls, and all our might.

Y

יָד YAD

Yad means "hand." When we read the Torah, we point to words with

a yad, a pointer made of metal, wood, or other material.

יְרוּשָׁלַיִם YERUSHALAYIM

Yerushalayim is the Hebrew name of the capital city of the State of Israel. The English name for Yerushalayim is Jerusalem.

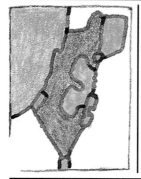

יִשְׂרָאֵל **YISRAEL**

Yisrael means "Israel." Yisrael is the people of Israel. Yisrael is the land of Israel.

יִזְכּוֹר **YIZKOR**

Yizkor means "God shall remember." It is a prayer Jews say to remember loved ones who have died.

יוֹם הָעַצְמָאוּת **YOM HA'ATZMAUT**

Israel Independence Day is Yom Ha'atzmaut. We celebrate the birthday of the State of Israel on Yom Ha'atzmaut.

יוֹם הַשׁוֹאָה **YOM HASHOAH**

Yom Hashoah is Holocaust Remembrance Day. On Yom Hashoah we remember the six million Jews who were murdered during World War II.

יוֹם כִּפּוּר   YOM KIPPUR

Yom Kippur is a holy day when we think about our behavior and how we can be nicer to others. Yom Kippur is a time for saying "I'm sorry."

יוֹם טוֹב   YOM TOV

Yom Tov means a "good day." We use the words Yom Tov to wish other Jews a happy holiday.

Z

זְמִירוֹת   ZEMIROT

Zemirot are "songs." We sing zemirot on Shabbat and at other happy times.